Life Around the World
School in Many Cultures

Heather Adamson

raintree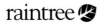

a Capstone company — publishers for children

Raintree is an imprint of Capstone Global Library Limited, a company incorporated in England and Wales having its registered office at 264 Banbury Road, Oxford, OX2 7DY – Registered company number: 6695582

www.raintree.co.uk
myorders@raintree.co.uk

Edited by Sarah L Schuette
Designed by Alison Thiele
Picture research by Kara Birr
Originated by Capstone Global Library Ltd
Printed and bound in China

ISBN 978 1 4747 3536 0
20 19 18 17 16
10 9 8 7 6 5 4 3 2 1

British Library Cataloguing in Publication Data
A full catalogue record for this book is available from the British Library.

Acknowledgements
Getty Images: Christina Sussman, 19; iStockphoto: davidf, 17, vinhdav, 11; Newscom: ABIR SULTAN/EPA, 7; Shutterstock: De Visu, 5, FredS, 1, Joseph Sohm, 13, Monkey Business Images, cover, Nadejda Ivanova, 15, Pressmaster, 9, 21

Contents

Places to learn

Students go to school
in many cultures.
How is your school
like other schools?

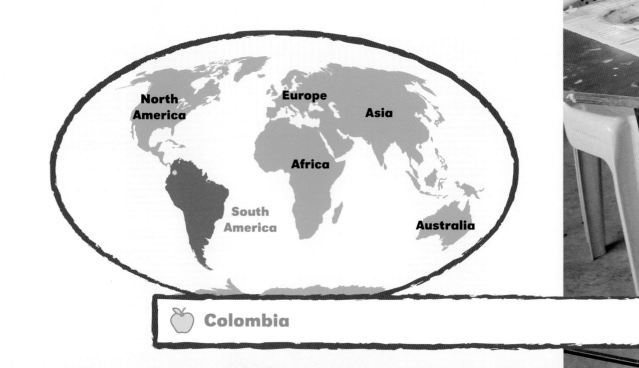

North
America

Europe

Asia

Africa

South
America

Australia

🍎 Colombia

Teachers work at school.

They teach many subjects.

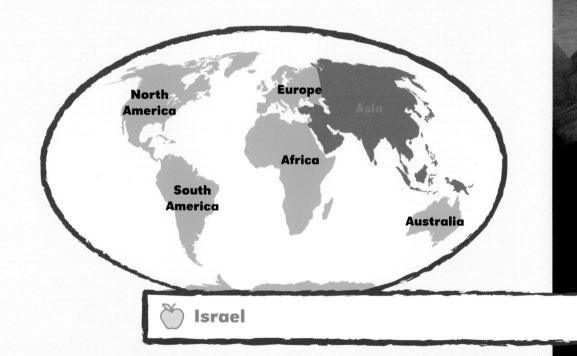

🍎 Israel

In class

Students learn in classrooms.
A girl in the United States
does maths on a blackboard.

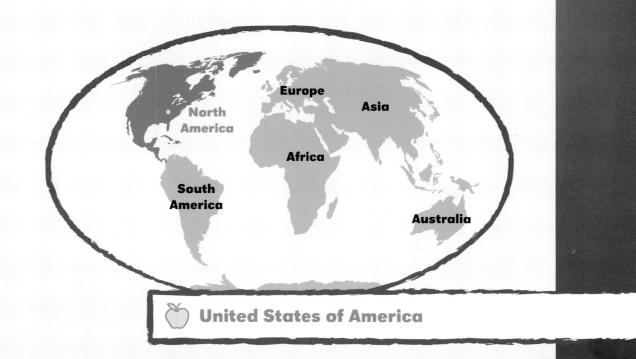

United States of America

9

Students learn outside.

A class in Vietnam studies

science and art at a park.

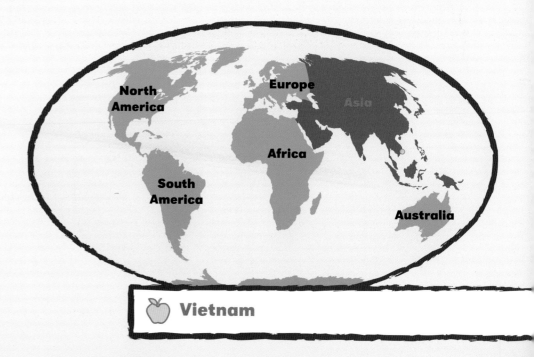

Students take notes.

A boy in Africa

listens to his teacher.

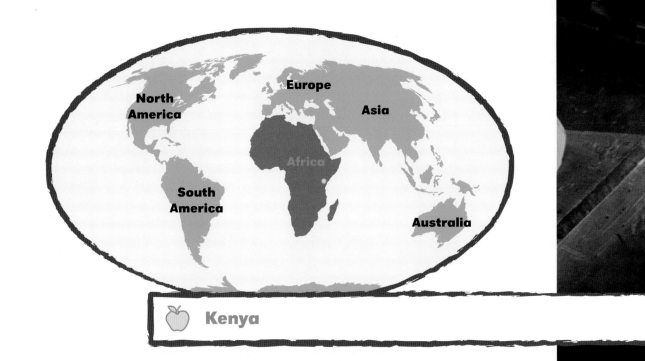

North
America

Europe

Asia

Africa

South
America

Australia

Kenya

Fun at school

Students go on field trips.

A class in France learns

about a castle.

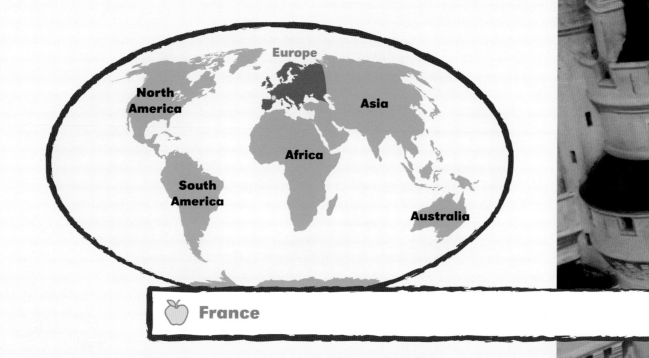

Europe

North America

Asia

Africa

South America

Australia

🍎 France

Students take lunch breaks.
Friends in Australia
eat together outside.

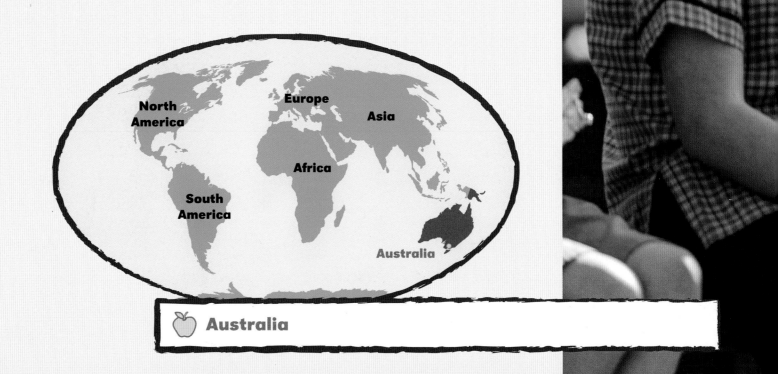

Australia

Students play at break time.

A girl in Africa skips.

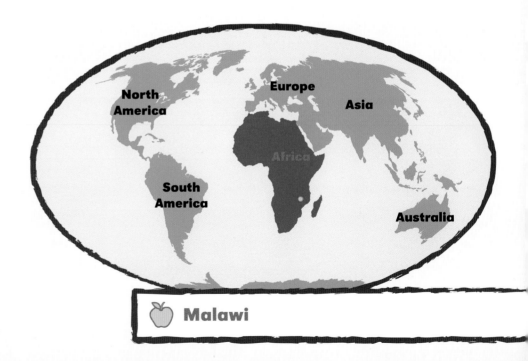

Your school

Around the world, students
laugh and learn at school.
Where do you go to school?

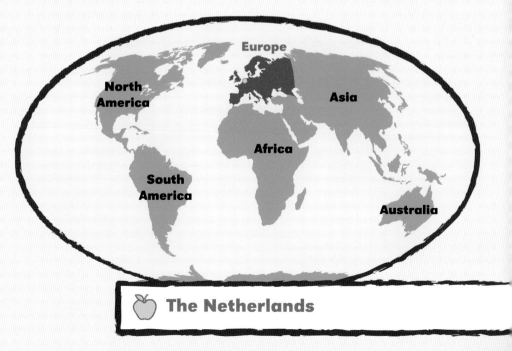

Glossary

classroom place where classes are taught; classrooms can be in buildings or outside

culture way of life, ideas, customs and traditions of a group of people

field trip trip to see and learn something new; classes often go on field trips to museums, zoos and other interesting places

maths study of numbers, shapes and measurements and how they relate to each other

science study of nature and the world

subject area of study; students learn subjects such as maths, science, art and music at school

Find out more

School Around the World (Time for Kids), Dona Herweck Rice (Teacher Created Materials, 2011)

School Days Around the World, Margriet Ruurs (Kids Can Press, 2015)

Schools Around the World (Children Like Us), Moira Butterfield (Wayland, 2016)

Websites

http://www.timeforkids.com/photos-video/slideshow/back-to-school-around-world/171326
Interesting photos of classrooms around the world.

https://www.theguardian.com/world/gallery/2015/oct/02/schools-around-the-world-un-world-teachers-day-in-pictures
Photos of schools in all different countries.

Index

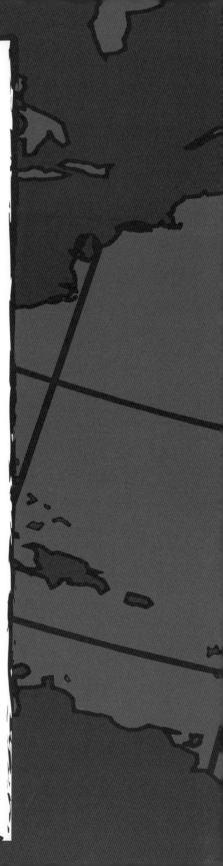